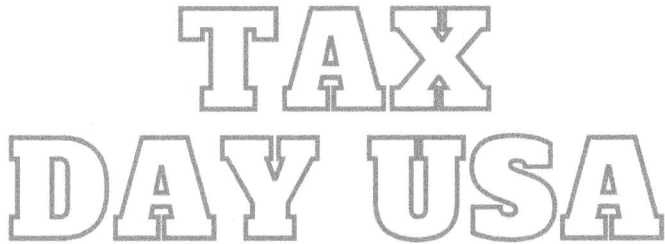

Created by Fabio MONTECHIESA

This coloring book is a space journey through the world of American taxes, with a touch of humor and sarcasm. Aliens, from distant planets, have settled in the United States and now must face their tax responsibilities. Here's what you'll find:

Paying Aliens: Images of aliens in formal attire, sitting at desks with calculators and tax forms. Some of them seem confused, while others are focused on filling out tax returns.

Dollar Trucks: Giant space trucks loaded with green dollars hurtle across the sky. These trucks deliver tax refunds to aliens who overpaid.

Interplanetary Tax Office: A futuristic building with a large "IRS" (Internal Revenue Service) sign welcomes aliens for their tax questions. The queues are long, and the aliens exchange advice on how to obtain tax deductions.

Space Sarcasm: Funny captions accompany the images. For example, an alien might say, "I have traveled across the universe, but nothing prepared me for the complexity of Earthly taxes!"

Vibrant Colors: Use your intergalactic markers to bring this world of taxes and aliens to life. Paint the stars, planets and numbers on the forms in bold colors.

In short, "Aliens and Dollars: Tax Week" is a coloring book that makes even the most dreaded time of the year fun: the tax return! 📷✂️

"Taxes are inevitable, like death. At least death doesn't come every year." - John Stossel

TAX DAY USA

"No one is patriotic when it comes to paying taxes." - George Orwell

TAX DAY USA

"There is always someone who is paid too much, and taxed too little – and it is always someone else."

TAX DAY USA

"Everyone seems normal until you get to know them. If you love someone, let them go. If he comes back, it means no one wanted him... Don't walk in front of me, I can't follow you. Don't walk behind, I'm not your guide. Don't even walk next to me. Just leave me alone."

TAX DAY USA

"Never give up on your dreams… sleep!"

TAX DAY USA

"Speaking is a skill of many. Listening is a virtue of few. Not understanding anything is a gift of many..."

TAX DAY USA

"Some people are like clouds, when they disappear it becomes a beautiful day."

TAX
DAY USA

"Taxes are like exams: you can't avoid them, but you can prepare as best you can!"

TAX DAY USA

"Paying taxes is like an annual subscription to adulthood. At least it doesn't come with a user manual!"

TAX DAY USA

"Remember, taxes are like a puzzle. If you solve them correctly, you win the 'Not Inspected' badge!"

TAX DAY USA

"Why did the accountant leave his calculator behind during tax season? He couldn't handle his complex emotions."

TAX DAY USA

"Tax Week: When Procrastination Meets Panic. But at least it's a workout for your stress-eating muscles!"

TAX DAY USA

"Taxes are like a game of hide and seek. The taxman is hiding, and we are looking for deductions!"

TAX DAY USA

"Why did the tax form go to therapy? He had too many issues to resolve."

TAX DAY USA

"In the grand scheme of the universe, taxes are just cosmic bureaucracy. So fill out those forms and be responsible as stardust!"

TAX DAY USA

TAX DAY USA

TAX DAY USA

TAX DAY USA

TAX DAY USA

TAX DAY USA

TAX DAY USA

©2024 F.M.
Created by Fabio Montechiesa
Illustrations through AI and image editing software.

"This work is published directly by the author through AMAZON's Kindle Direct Publishing self-publishing platform and the author owns all rights to it exclusively. Therefore, no part of this book may be reproduced without the prior consent of the author." (ydefix84@gmail.com)